TO HAVE & TO HOLD

WELCOME HOME
LONNIE!
~WANT YA TO MEET MY GIRL, KATE!
AIN'T SHE A HONEY?

FOR EDDIE COYLE AND POPEYE DOYLE
AND ALL THE OTHER GUYS
WHO THOUGHT THEY COULD BEAT THE HOUSE

~IOWA GOVERNOR NORMAN ERBE REFUSED TODAY TO STAY THE EXECUTION OF CONVICTED SLAYER CHARLES EDMUND KELLY...

~AT THE WHITE HOUSE, PRESIDENT KENNEDY HAS DECLARED THAT THE UNITED STATES WILL USE WHATEVER MEANS NECESSARY TO BLOCK AN OFFENSIVE ARMS BUILDUP IN CUBA..

YOU BROKE MY HEART 'CAUSE I COULDN'T DANCE ~ ♫ DIDN'T EVEN WANT ME AROUND... ♪
POND

DO YOU LOVE ME? ♫♪ I CAN REALLY MOVE
DO YOU LOVE ME? ♪♪ I'M IN THE GROOVE...

?

WHOA NELLIE!
WHAT ARE YOU SO DOLLED UP FOR?
CAN'T I LOOK NICE?

SURE! ~YOU LOOK PRETTY NICE TO ME!
LONNIE DON'T!
~HEY!
QUIT!
~YOU'LL MESS MY MAKEUP!

BESIDES ~ YOU'LL BE LATE FOR WORK.

WHAT ARE YOU TALKING ABOUT? TRAFFIC'S LIGHT THIS TIME OF NIGHT ~ I GOT PLENTY OF TIME.
NO YOU DON'T, MISTER SMARTYPANTS - BECAUSE I NEED THE CAR. IT'S BINGO NIGHT AT ST. DOM'S ~ REMEMBER?

~BUT~
IT WON'T KILL YOU TO TAKE THE TRAIN ~ STOP'S RIGHT DOWNTOWN...

SONUVA ~ WHY'NT YOU SAY SOMETHING EARLIER? NOW I WILL BE LATE!

NOT IF YOU HURRY.
KEYS.

CHRIST...
~HERE!
SMACK!

~YER A PAIN IN THE ASS, KATE ~ YOU KNOW THAT, RIGHT?
SO BUY A SECOND CAR ~ WE NEED ONE...

ON WHAT I PULL IN? DON'T MAKE ME LAUGH.
WELL, AND WHOSE FAULT IS THAT?

SLAM!

~DON'T START WITH ME ON THAT CAN OF WORMS! I'D BEAT YER ASS, BUT I AIN'T GOT THE TIME...
SO ~ GO ALREADY!

300
METR
PLA

METROPOLITAN FIDUCIARY
MF
PROGRESS + PRUDENCE
FOR A SECURE FUTURE
TO HAVE & TO HOLD
by Graham Chaffee

NICK'S SUNRISE
CAFE

SEAT YOURSELF

ONE EARLY-BIRD! ONE CORNED BEEF!
?

IRIS?
?
IRIS

~WHY, LONNIE ROSS AS I LIVE AN' BREATHE!

SO WHAT BRINGS YOU DOWN HERE THIS TIME OF DAY?
OH~ I JUST PULLED A NIGHT-SHIFT OVER AT THE MET-FI BUILDING. NORMALLY, I'D DRIVE IN, BUT KATE NEEDED THE CAR FOR~

OH, HOW IS KATE, THESE DAYS? WE NEVER SEE HER DOWN AT ST. DOM'S, NO MORE!
ORDER UP!
OH. ~UH... SHE'S FINE.

GOOD, GOOD...
ORDER UP!
I GOT IT! ~SHEESH...
LISSEN, LONNIE, I GOTTA RUN BUT YOU SAY HELLO FOR ME TO KATE! ~TELL HER NOT TO BE SUCH A STRANGER!
YOU WANT A DONUT OR SOMETHIN'?
ER~ ~NO THANKS, IRIS ~ I BETTER HEAD HOME...
IRIS

WELL, IT WAS GREAT RUNNING INTO YA AGAIN! STOP BY MORE OFTEN, NOW YA KNOW I'M HERE!
HAMBURGER ····· 60¢
BACON & TOMATO ··· 50¢
BAKED HAM & CHEESE 60¢
HAM/EGG SALAD ···· 50¢
Try Our MALTED MILK!
WILL DO!

SO...
~HOW WAS BINGO?

HAVE A GOOD TIME?
~MN...

WIN MUCH?
?

YEAH ~ WE'RE FRIGGIN MILLIONAIRES!
~WILL YOU SHUT THE HELL UP?

... JESUS...

WHA?..

MPH~GET OFF...
CHRIST!

WHAT THE HELL HAS GOTTEN INTO YOU, LATELY?

NOTHIN'. NEVERMIND.

YOU KNOW I GOTTA' BE AT WORK IN A COUPLE HOURS, RIGHT?
~MHN.

~ WHAT'S **EATING** YOU, ANYWAYS?

~ SOMETHING HAPPEN I SHOULD KNOW ABOUT?
HUH?
~ NO... LIKE WHAT?

YOU TELL ME!
~YOU'RE THE ONE FUMBLING AROUND LIKE A KID, AT THE CRACK OF DAWN!
~I **TOLD** YA, IT'S NOTHING...
~JUST A LITTLE WOUND UP, IS ALL...

"WOUND UP", HUH?...
FORGET IT.

DON'T GET ALL POUTY.
ALRIGHT ALREADY! DROP IT!

SIGH WELL...
WHOA! ~KATE!

WHAT?
THIS IS WHAT YOU WANTED, RIGHT? ~YOU GONNA' COMPLAIN, NOW?

NO, BUT...
THAT'S WHAT I THOUGHT...

HUH.
THERE NOW...

THAT OUGHTTA' SETTLE YOU DOWN.
PHEW...

I'M GONNA' GO WASH UP...

~YOU'RE WELCOME.

COPA
CLUB

FLUSH

Z Z Z Z Z Z

DORFMANNS
DORFM

MAGIC CASTLE
PAGODA

WHAT?!

YESSIR!
WHAM!
~ANNND, HE PICKS UP THE SPARE! NOT BAD, HUH?
~YOU SEE THAT?
YEAH. SWELL.
Gus
Mr. T's BOWL
LOTTA GUYS WOULDN'T HAVE THE STONES TO EVEN TRY FOR THAT SPLIT...
CHILDREN
FRIDAY: LADIES
LEAGUE
~BUT I HAD A FEELING IN MY GUT, Y'KNOW?
~THAT'S THE SECRET, BUDDY...
CONFIDENCE!

~CONFIDENCE...

Mr. T's FAMILY B

1

2

3

~YA GOTTA BE **SURE**...

ALMOST DIDN'T RECOGNIZE YA WITHOUT A UNIFORM, "DETECTIVE"...
GET USED TO IT.

7th PRECINCT
RING!
RING!
POLICE
MPD

FERGUSEN.
OH-HEY BUDDY~LONG TIME! HOW'S THE SECURITY BUSINESS TREATING YA?
UH HUH.
YOU GOT THAT RIGHT...
UH HUH...

OH~SAME OLD STORY, YOU KNOW HOW IT IS...
YEAH...
HUH? YEAH? INNA' SHOP HUH? THAT'S A BITCH...

HUH? OH SURE~SHOULDN'T BE A PROBLEM~YEAH~JUST GO DOWN TO THE IMPOUND AND PICK ONE UP... I'LL TELL KELLY TO EXPECT YOU... HUH?~NAH...
HE OWES ME A FAVOR ANYWAY...
NOTICE
PLEASE DO NOT
REMEMBER
ALL PERSONS USING
MUST
BY 1000
7254

SURE, I'M SURE! HEY~YOU STILL GOT PLENTY OF FRIENDS, DOWN HERE. "ONCE A COP~ALWAYS A COP" AMIRIGHT?
YOU SHOULD COME DOWN~SAY HELLO~GRAB A FEW BEERS...
RELEASE
MAR.-APR.
COOK CO
DIRECT
19

I'LL DO THAT, FERG. THANKS~YER A PAL...

HEY, MITT ~ LONNIE ~ SAY, CAN I GET YA TO COVER FOR ME, THURSDAY? ... YEAH... 8:00 TO 6:00 AT THE MET-FI, DOWNTOWN... YEAH... THANKS ~ I OWE YA ONE...
HEH ~ I'M SURE YOU WILL...

SIGH...
CLUNK

YAWN

FIDUCIARY
PROGRESS + PRU
FOR A SECURE FU
YOU MISSED A SPOT.
FUCK YOU, MAN.

SO DID YOU NOTICE HOW MANY EXCUSES DORIS FINDS FOR STAYING LATE?
MM-HM... A "SPECIAL PROJECT" FOR MR. DEHUNE.

OH, I'M SURE HE FINDS HER ASSISTANCE INVALUABLE!
GIGGLE!

SERIOUSLY THOUGH, SHE NEEDS TO WATCH OUT...

IF SHE THINKS THERE'S A FUTURE WITH HIM, SHE'S GOT ANOTHER THINK COMING...

~WOULDN'T BE THE FIRST GIRL DISAPPOINTED BY A MAN.

RING!
RING!
LONNIE!
RING!
!!
RING!
GODDAMMIT!
LONNIE!
RING!
ALL RIGHT ALREADY...
RING!
WHAT!? ~OH, HI, JUNE...
NO, NO. I WAS JUST IN THE BATH...
GETTING DOLLED UP FOR "BINGO NIGHT?"
WE'RE MEETING AT THE COPA.
AGAIN.
FANCY!
YEAH...
~ I DUNNO, JUNE... THINK I'M MAKING A MISTAKE?
MISTAKE?
HOW DO YOU MEAN?
~HE'S RICH AND HANDSOME, ISN'T HE?
SURE SURE, BUT...

~ YOU'RE HAVING A GOOD TIME, RIGHT?
~ WHAT MORE COULD YA WANT?

OKAY, TUCK... TIME TO STEP UP...

SO WHAT'RE YOU AND THE GIRLS UP TO TONIGHT?
BINGO?
MAH-JONGG.

ALRIGHT ~ SEE YA, TOMORROW.
YUP.

AVE BRIDGE ONLY
25

PER
INN
RED'S
CLAM
SHACK
BEER

COPA

LBC-670

BBQ

MOTEL
AIR CONDITIONED
VACANCY

13

VEHICLE
REGISTRATION

13

OH OH..

OH!
OH!
OH!

HA HA HA
AH!

~WHEW... OKAY, STUD. THAT WAS SOMETHING.
~NOW GET OFF ME AND FIX US A DRINK, WHYDONCHA?

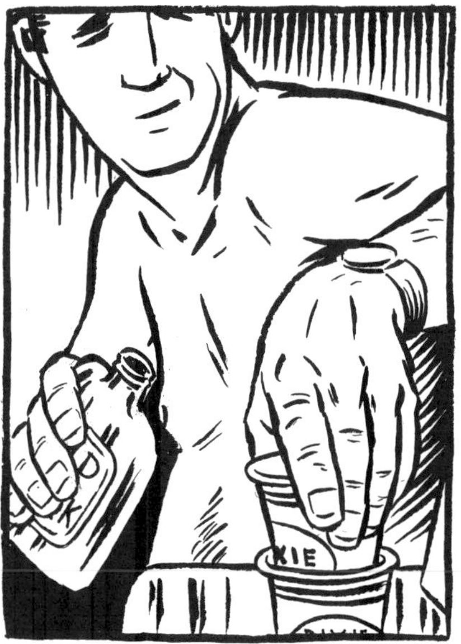

CHEERS.

SO ~ BIG SPENDER...
WHAT IS THIS DUMP?
COME HERE OFTEN?

OH, I DUNNO...
~RIGHT ON THE SHORE.
~CLOSE TO THE COPA...
IT'S - YOU KNOW...
CONVENIENT.

IS THAT WHAT THIS IS? "CONVENIENT?"
... GOT AN OCEAN VIEW...

I WAS THINKING...

WOULDN'T IT BE NICE TO HAVE A PLACE IN THE CITY?
A PLACE OF OUR OWN?...

-DON'T GET ME WRONG... THESE LITTLE TRYSTS ARE FUN, BUT...

WHOA NOW-HEH HEH ~ I DON'T KNOW IF...

IF WHAT?
~I'M NOT SOME LITTLE CHIPPY YOU CAN IMPRESS WITH YOUR FANCY PAPER CUPS FROM THE BOBCAT MOTOR-INN!
BIP

EASY, TIGER! ~I'LL TELL YOU WHAT; NEXT TIME, WE'LL GET A ROOM AT THE PIEDMONT. CHAMPAGNE, ROOM-SERVICE...
~HOW DOES THAT GRAB YOU?
"NEXT TIME?" I DUNNO, TUCK. I REALLY DON'T...

IT MIGHT NOT BE "CONVENIENT."

AW KATE, C'MON NOW...
MM-HM.
~ MAYBE.
~ MAYBE NOT...

ROMANCE IS A MYSTERY.

12

COMING SOON
ROSEWOOD
SHOPPING CENTER
ANTIQUES
REST HAVEN MOTEL
9

BEACON HOTEL
ERMO
PARKING

ST. MORITZ
WIGS
NOVELTIES
CLOSED

PAT'S TAP

BEER.
CHEERS, BUD.

SAY ~ IS THAT YOUR BENZ, OUTSIDE?
THAT'S A NICE CAR!
~BET THE GIRLS GO NUTS FOR A CAR LIKE THAT AMIRIGHT?
WELL, HEH...
I GUESS IT DOESN'T HURT ANY.

BETCHER ASS IT DOESN'T...
SKIRTS LOVE A NICE RIDE...
TRUTH.
~YOU CAN TAKE THAT TO THE BANK.

FUNNY YOU SHOULD SAY THAT 'CAUSE THAT'S JUST WHAT I DO...
~TAKE IT TO THE BANK; I'M A LOANS MANAGER OVER AT FIRST-FEDERAL IN TARRYTOWN.

~HUH ~ HOW 'BOUT THAT?

SO TELL ME ~ WHAT'S A GUY WITH A CAR LIKE THAT, DOING IN A PLACE LIKE THIS?
HM?
I MEAN - SHOULDN'T YA BE AT A COUNTRY CLUB? ~ SOMEPLACE WITH DECENT LIQUOR?

HEH, HEH ~ EVEN BANKERS HAVE TO CUT LOOSE, NOW AND THEN. ~SEE A LITTLE NIGHT LIFE...
BESIDES...

THIS PLACE HAS A CERTAIN... SOMETHING.
~IT'S SOMETHING ALL RIGHT...

WHAT ABOUT YOU? WHAT DO YOU DO?
ME? I'M IN PRIVATE SECURITY...

HELPING FOLKS HOLD ONTO WHAT BELONGS TO THEM.

WELP ~ THAT DOES IT FOR ME. TIME FOR BEDDY~BYE...

NICE TO MEETCHA MR ~ ER...

MARTIN ~ TUCKER MARTIN. MY FRIENDS CALL ME TUCK.
HERE'S MY CARD.

WELL, NICE TALKIN' TO YA, TUCK ~ SEE YA AROUND.
~ DON'T DRIVE TOO FAST!
I WON'T HA-HA!

I'D HATE TO HAVE TO READ ABOUT YA IN THE PAPERS!

FIRST FEDERAL...

~SMALL WORLD.

CLUNK

SLAM

HEH.

~ENJOY IT WHILE IT LASTS, BABY...
TUCKER MARTIN
LOANS MANAGER
IRST FEDERAL SAVINGS & LOAN

IT'S ALL ABOUT HAVING A STRATEGY...
~LISTEN TO HIM, THE NAPOLEON OF CANASTA.

FYD-
FINNOCCI'S
FIRST FEDERAL SAVINGS&LOAN
FIDELITY
THERE IS A GOD...
I KNEW WE COVERED THIS PLACE.

FIND WHAT YOU WERE LOOKING FOR, MR. ROSS?
RECORDS
SURE DID, STELLA~THANKS FOR LETTING ME POKE AROUND.
JOHN COMPANY SECURITY
DELIVERIES AT MAIN ENTRANCE ON 3RD AVE

JEFF KRUGER'S
JAZZ AT THE
Flamingo
CHRIST, LONNIE. ~DO YOU KNOW WHAT TIME IT IS?
ONE IN THE AFTERNOON.
~MEET ME DOWNSTAIRS; I GOT SOMETHING I WANNA TALK TO YOU ABOUT.
I KNOW THIS IS A BAD IDEA...
~JUST PUT YER PANTS ON AND COME ON DOWN.

MEIN · NOODLES
FISH · SALAD
~IT'S ONE OF THOSE MODERN LAYOUTS~ WIDE OPEN, EVERYONE VISIBLE ALL THE TIME.
SAMWO
813
OPEN
HOURS DAILY
11AM - 3AM
CLOSED ON SUNDAY
WE'RE IN WE'RE OUT NO MUSS NO FUSS.
WHAT ABOUT ALARMS?
SIMPLE BELL SYSTEM, NOTHING WE CAN'T CONTROL...
THE GUARD'S ONE OF OUR "GRAY BRIGADE" HE'S ABOUT 75 YEARS OLD...
I'M TELLIN' YA ROY...
IT'S LIKE THEY WANT TO BE KNOCKED OVER.
IT'S A CAKEWALK!
~KEEP IT DOWN, WILLYA?
JESUS-WILL YOU RELAX? NOBODY IN THIS DUMP GIVES A FUCK WHAT WE TALK ABOUT.

I DUNNO, LONNIE..
SURE, SURE. ~YOU'RE NERVOUS.
NERVOUS ~ WHAT THE HELL, LONNIE? WE'VE NEVER DONE ANYTHING REMOTELY LIKE THIS ~ EVER!
AND WHATEVER YOU SAY...
I'M PRETTY SURE ROBBING A BANK ISN'T A "CAKEWALK!"
CALM DOWN.

WHAT REALLY MAKES ME NERVOUS IS HOW GODDAMNED CONFIDENT YOU ARE...

REMEMBER HOW WELL THE LAST "EASY" SCORE WORKED OUT?

SIGH...

LOOK...
JUST BECAUSE WE'VE NEVER DONE THIS BEFORE DOESN'T MAKE IT IMPOSSIBLE.
~AND WHEN THAT OTHER SHIT WENT DOWN, I TOOK IT STANDING UP, DIDN'T I?
~NEVER MENTIONED YOU.
~NEVER SAID A WORD...

~FIGURED I OWED YA ONE ON ACCOUNT OF ME MARRYING KATE AND ALL...

POINT IS...
YOU CAN TRUST ME ON THIS...
THIS IS A REAL 'OPPORTUNITY KNOCKS' TYPE THING HERE, ROY.

HEY~WHY YOU NOT FINISH?
YOU NOT LIKE, HAH?

YOU KIDDIN? THIS SHIT TASTES LIKE A TIRE.
HAH? WHAT YOU SAY? 渾蛋!

YOU DON'T LIKE IT, YOU NOT GOTTA STAY HERE, FATTY! 窩囊廢
JEEZ, LONNIE...
CHECK PLEASE!
YOU CAN GO!
王八...

HEH HEH.

I KNOW A DRIVER WE COULD USE...
MAYBE.

WELL ALLRIGHT!
~I KNEW YA WOULDN'T LET ME DOWN!
THIS GUY LOCAL?
REASONABLY.
WELL, GIVE HIM A CALL WHYDONTCHA?

WE CAN PICK HIM UP AT HIS PLACE, NOW.

汤

SO...
~WHAT'S GOT YOU INTERESTED IN BANKS ALL OF A SUDDEN?
OH... I GOT MY REASONS...

ESTHER! ~I GOTTA GO OUT A MINUTE.
~SEE ROY 'BOUT SOMETHIN'...
CLUNK
YOUR DINNER'S ALMOST READY. CAN'T YOU SEE ROY SOME OTHER TIME?

'SIDES... YOU GONNA LIKE WHAT I FIXED FOR DESSERT...

THAT GONNA HAVE TO WAIT. HE'S ALREADY DRIVIN' OVER.

WHY? WHAT'S SO IMPORTANT ALL OF A SUDDEN?
BUSINESS.

WELL, I KNOW WHATEVER BUSINESS THAT ROY IS ABOUT, IS BAD BUSINESS...
~HE IS NOT WELCOME IN MY HOME!

YOU CAN WAIT FOR ROY ON THE PORCH!

TUCKER MARTIN

ACCOUNTS ~ OH, HELLO, MR MARTIN... WHAT CAN WE DO FOR YOU TODAY?

WELL... I HAVE SOME GOOD NEWS ~ REGARDING THAT MATTER WE SPOKE OF LAST WEEK...
WHAT? OUR OWN PLACE?
YUP!
TAPPITY TAP

ON THE LEVEL? YOU'RE NOT JUST PULLING MY CHAIN?
SCOUT'S HONOR!
WHEN CAN I SEE IT?

UH-HUH ... AFTER THE FIRST...
PAINTERS...UH-HUH.
YOU **HAVE** BEEN A BUSY BOY!

ALL THAT HARD WORK DESERVES A **REWARD** ...
HAVE YOU HAD YOUR LUNCH, YET?
~ WELL **DON'T**...
I THINK WE'LL HAVE TO MAKE AN EXTRA CASH DEPOSIT, THIS WEEK...

TAKE A LEFT OVER THE BRIDGE...
BUTCHERTOWN ~ HE'S A SPOOK, THIS FRIEND OF YOURS?

HE'S A GOOD GUY.
SURE SURE...

THERE HE IS NOW.

SUPER
SOUL KIT
STOP

H'LO, ROY.
CALVIN, LONNIE. LONNIE, CALVIN.
~NICE TO MEETCHA, CALVIN.
HOP IN.

SO, CALVIN ~ DID ROY FILL YOU IN?

MAN, YOU LOOK LIKE A COP.

DO I? HUH ~ YEAH, GUESS I DO...
~MUST BE ALL THOSE YEARS I SPENT AS A COP.
MAN ~ I KNEW IT! FUCK YOU, ROY, ~ I'M OUT!
HEH HEH...
TAKE IT EASY! LONNIE'S NOT A COP! ~NOBODY HERE'S A COP ANYMORE!

WHATCHOO MEAN "NOT A COP ANYMORE"?
~SOUND LIKE BULLSHIT, MAN...
IT MEANS I WAS A COP, ONCE...
LIQUO
ICE

~ BUT NOW I'M IN BUSINESS STRICTLY FOR MYSELF.

~ALL RIGHT, HERE WE ARE...
PARK
1ST FEDERAL BANK
57
1ST FEDERAL BANK
~LET'S GO INSIDE AND TAKE A LOOK AROUND.

CHANGE FOR A $20, PLEASE.
CERTAINLY SIR.

DUPAR
RARE COINS
STAMPS
NUMISMATIST
MIND YO BUSINESS, LADY.

WHY
SAVE?

SEE ENOUGH?
IT'LL DO.

HERE ~ YOU DRIVE...

~ PRACTICE OUR "GETAWAY."
TAXI

MAKE YOUR NEXT RIGHT...

~ TAKE THE EXPRESSWAY TO WILLETTE...

HERE YA GO.
TAXI

24 HOUR TOW
SHORTY'S
~ I GOT A PLACE IN MIND...

DEPOSIT FOR DORFMANN'S DEPARTMENT STORE.

WHAT ABOUT THE CAR?
I GOT THAT.
GONNA NEED CLEAN PLATES...

TOLD YOU ~ I GOT THAT SHIT **COVERED.**

I'LL TAKE MY LUNCH HOUR NOW, ALICE...

ALL RIGHT ~ WE MEET BACK HERE TUESDAY MORNING, AND DO THIS THING.

YOUR DINNER'S COLD.

HELLO, HANDSOME!
HUNGRY?

THIS HAS BEEN THE WEIRDEST DAY...
TIME FOR A DRINK.

BEER
LIQU
SPIR
IES
BEER
SODAS
OPEN

BEER
LIQUOR
SPIRITS
HEY...
HALLOWEEN
SALE

TER HOTEL

WHAT.
WE'RE GONNA NEED DISGUISES...
~BACK IN A MINUTE.

WHAT THE HELL IS THIS?
YOU WANNA BE THE CAT OR THE DOG?

YOU'RE OVER AN **HOUR LATE** MRS. ROSS!
THERE WAS A LINE AT THE BANK.

CALL YA IN A COUPLE DAYS.
OKE.

KINDA' LATE AREN'T YA?
MN...
WHAT'S FOR DINNER?
CHINESE.
JADE PALACE RESTAURANT

HAD IT FOR LUNCH.

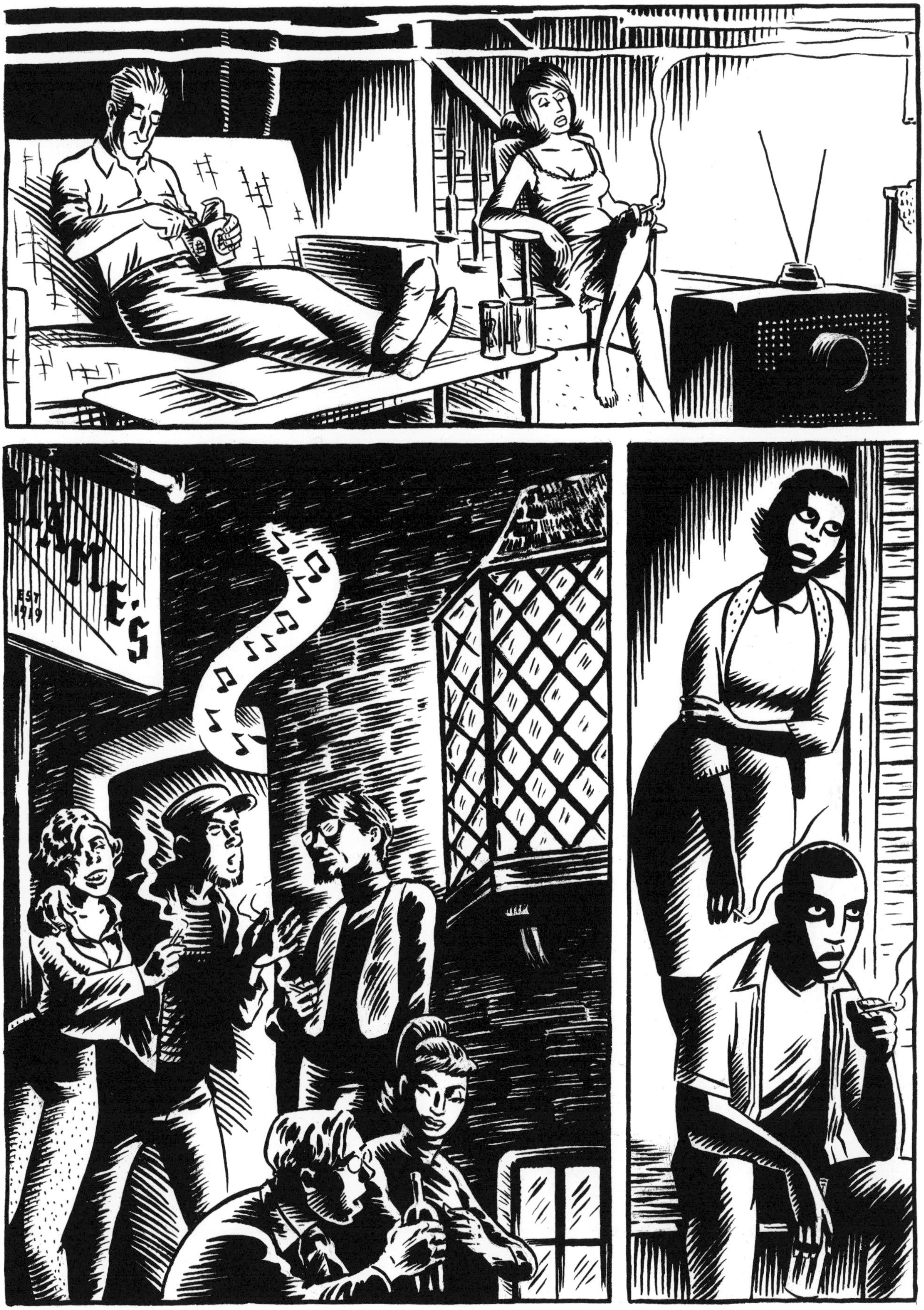

I TALKED TO MARY AT WORK, TODAY...
MM?
~HER COUSIN WORKS DOWN AT THE CANNERY.
SHE SAID THEY HIRING.

HIRING?
~BABY, I GOT A JOB!

HELPING THAT OL' DRUNK AT THE SALVAGE YARD?
THAT AIN'T NO JOB!

~NOT TALKIN' BOUT NO SALVAGE YARD.
~AND NO CANNERY BULLSHIT, NEITHER...

THIS IS BIG MONEY.
WHAT DO YOU MEAN, "BIG MONEY"?

GONNA BE RICH.

MAME'S

RRRRRRRRRR

RRRRRRRR

BODY FENDER
PAINT & GLASS
WORK
Chrysler

ZZZZZZ~RING!

RED'S...
NO.

YAWN

THOUGHT I TOLD YOU TO PART THAT UP LAST WEEK.
I'LL DO IT NEXT WEEK...

~GOT A USE FOR IT, MEANTIMES.
WHATCHOO NEED A CAR FOR, BOY?

YOU GOIN' SOMEPLACE?
A VACATION?

WHERE YOU GOIN'?
PLANNING TO DRIVE DOWN TO BRAZIL?

~GET YOU SOME OF THAT BRAZILIAN POON~TASTE LIKE BANANAS 'N' SHIT?
DOES ESTHER KNOW?

SOMEBODY GONNA' BE SLEEPIN' OUTDOORS...

I NEED IT TO ROB A BANK.
~WELL, OF COURSE YOU DO!..
~HOW YOU EXPECT THOSE BRAZILIAN LADIES TO GIVE UP THEY BANANAS WITHOUT SOME READY CASH?
THAT'S JUST COMMON SENSE...

SLAM!

RRR~

VROOM!

U-STORE

SO WHATTAYA THINK? CAN WE COUNT ON THIS NEGRO BUDDY OF YOURS TO DELIVER?
AIRY

UH HUH.
AND THE CAR?
SO WE'RE SET, THEN...
YOU ALL RIGHT?

YEAH ~ JUST A LITTLE JITTERY.
~ I'LL BE FINE.
YEAH.
HERE'S TO CRIME! - HEH...

HERE YA GO.
TOOK YA LONG ENOUGH

~ WHAT ARE **YOU** LOOKING SO PLEASED ABOUT?

YOU KNOW SOMETHING I DON'T KNOW?

I DUNNO...

~YOU TELL **ME**.

BELCH!

~LIKE WHAT?

MRS. O'CONNELL'S DONE A DECENT JOB WITH THOSE ROSE BUSHES.

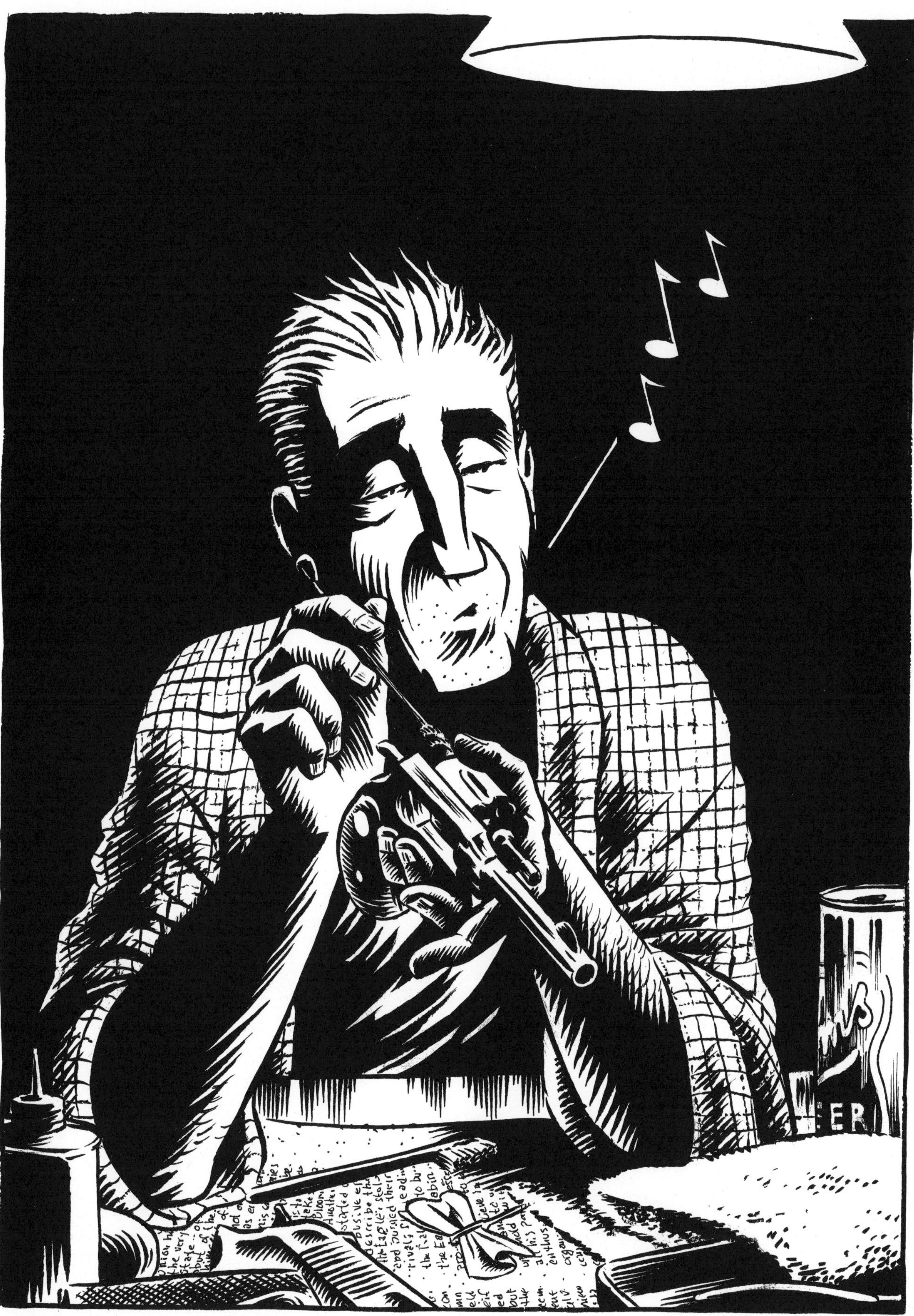

DER
RILLS
W
SCOOTA BOATS
10 ¢
HOST
OUSE
DUNNO WHAT YOU TWO GENIUSES ARE UP TO, OVER HERE, BUT IT'S STARTING...
RELAX, WILLYA? WE'LL BE RIGHT THERE...

KZUN
DIAL 630
MOFFAT'S
MEANS Quality!

24 HOUR TOW
SHORTY'S

Ford
IN YOUR FUTURE
GEO. WILKINSON CO
SHOES · LUGGAGE
SPORTING GOODS
LAWRENCE AND SON FINANCE
RESTAURANT
Mayfield's
SASSO
PRINCE EDWARD HOTEL

BURRITT
TQP112

ANY MINUTE NOW...
~THERE WE GO...

OPEN FOR BUSINESS. THAT'S OUR CUE.

~OKAY, CALVIN~JUST CIRCLE THE BLOCK ONCE AND THEN WAIT FOR US AT THE SIDE...
~I KNOW MY JOB, MAN!
~ALL RIGHT--RELAX...

~ROLL UP SLOWLY...

LET'S DO THIS.

FIRST FEDERAL BANK

ALL RIGHT! STICK 'EM UP, PEOPLE!

THIS IS A ROBBERY!

I WANT EVERYBODY TO MOVE TO THE BACK OF THE ROOM!

KEEP IT COOL...

OH DEAR.

LET'S GET THE DOOR ALL LOCKED UP, HUH POPS?

SNATCH

PARK

25C

Come in
we're Open

ALL RIGHT~ C'MON, TUCK. LET'S GET THE VAULT OPEN.
HUH?

I CAN'T~ IT- IT'S ON A TIMELOCK.
NO IT ISN'T.
GET BUSY.

ATTABOY...

GOT ALL THE SMALL STUFF?
YUP.

WELL, GET IN THERE AND GO TO TOWN, KITTY!
MEOW!

GOT IT. LET'S GO.
GO ON. I'LL WAIT 'TIL YER OUT...

OKAY ~ EVERYBODY INTO THE VAULT.
HUH? BUT-

~BECAUSE SIMON SAYS SO!
~NOW GO ON.

C'MON ROY...

SHOVE ALONG THERE, FOLKS.
~PLENTY OF ROOM...

WE'RE JUST ABOUT DONE HERE...

?

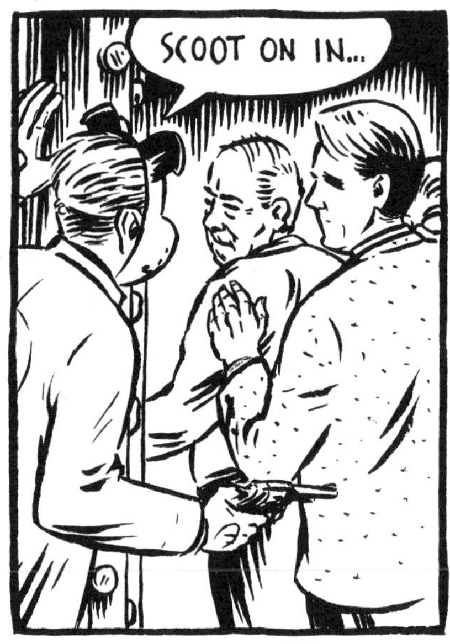
SCOOT ON IN...

?

SWELL.

THAT'S ALICE.
~MY SECRETARY.
HELLO?
FIRST FEDERAL
KNOCK
KNOCK

WELL HECK~ LET HER IN, TUCK!

HURRY UP ~ AND DON'T BE STUPID, OR THIS ENDS IN TEARS.
OK, OK...

~THE HELL?
GOTCHA!

BLAM!
OH SHIT!
THAT'S **IT** MAN...
~WE'RE **OUTTA'** HERE!
~NO NO **WAIT!** THERE HE IS!
HURRY UP!

WHAT THE HELL WAS THAT?
GO, GO, GO!
I'M GOING!
VROOOM!

HA-HA-HA~WHEW!
~LONNIE! WHAT WAS THAT? WE HEARD SHOTS!

SHOT.
~YOU HEARD A SHOT...
~SHOT-SHOTS, WHAT'S THE DIFFERENCE?!
~'S MESSED UP, MAN!
JUST DRIVE.

LOOK~ HE WENT FOR MY GUN.
~ WHAT WAS I SUPPOSED TO DO FOR CHRISSAKES?
SHOOTING PEOPLE WAS NEVER PART OF THE PLAN IS WHAT I'M SAYING...
DO YOU THINK YA **KILLED** HIM?

I'M LEAVING FOR THE BANK, NOW...
DON'T BE ALL DAY.

~AND THEN HE SAID, "LET HER IN, TUCK." ~ OR SOMETHING LIKE THAT.
~AND BARNEY GRABBED HIS ARM AND HE SHOT HIM.
~HE CALLED THE GUARD "TUCK?"

NO~HE WAS SPEAKING TO OUR BRANCH MANAGER, MR. MARTIN...
HIS FIRST NAME IS TUCKER.
TUCKER.

~AND THIS WAS RIGHT AFTER YOU ENTERED THE VAULT... IS THAT CORRECT?
YES.
..."TQP" SOMETHIN' ...

AND HE CALLED YOU, "TUCK" IS THAT CORRECT?
CALLED YOU BY NAME?
WELL, YES ~ I GUESS HE DID...
~SIR, DO YOU KNOW THIS MAN?
WHAT? NO!
~IT'S UH...

THIS PAPER, SIR...
~SEEMS TO BE A PRETTY DETAILED MAP OF THE BANK...
OH MY!
~FLOORPLAN, EXITS, ALARMS...
STAFF LOUNGE
BR
ALARMS?
2ND ALARM HERE
VAULT
2 ALARMS HERE
GUARD

YESSIR ~ FOUND IT ON THE FLOOR OF THE VAULT...
DO YOU KNOW ANYTHING ABOUT THIS, SIR?

WHAT?
AH ~ NO... I'VE NEVER SEEN THAT BEFORE...
~LISTEN, ABOUT MY NAME...
LIEUTENANT, WE GOT A GUY SEZ HE CAN MAYBE I.D. THE CAR.

~MY NAME...
EXCUSE ME, SIR.

IT'S JUST...
~ IT'S ON THE NAMEPLATE...
ON MY DESK...
TUCKER MAR

?

WHAT THE HELL?
METRO CAB

FEDER
NK

MA'AM...
OH, GET A JOB
~MR. MARTIN!

OH ~ ER ~ MRS. ROSS!
WHAT'S GOING ON?
A ~ UM... ROBBERY.
WHAT?

I ~ UH ~ I HAVE TO GO ~ TO THE STATION... MAKE A STATEMENT...
OH...

H'LO, KATE.

TOM?
EYY~MRS. R!

WOTTA MESS, HUH?

24 HOUR TOW
SHORTYS

SALEM
FRUIT
lem Fruit Co

GREYHOUND
THIS IS GOOD...

~I'LL CATCH A BUS BACK INTO THE CITY.
ZIP..

YOU SURE?
SURE, I'M SURE.
THAT'S A LOTTA DOUGH TO CARRY...
I'M A BIG BOY.

OH YEAH...

HERE...
BETTER TAKE THIS BACK.

SEE YA 'ROUND.
DON'T GET ROBBED.

GREYHOUND
METROPOLITAN DAILY NEWS

DEPARTURES

PLAY IT
SAFE
NOTICE

GREYHOUND

TEASLEYS

SANFORD AUTO SALVAGE
NOTICE
DO NOT REMOVE ANY PARTS UNTIL PAID For SEE MGR FIRST
OFFICE
TQP112

CONES
PLANE
DETECTIVE
MYSTIC
POPULAR MECHANIC
TIME

WON IT AT THE TRACK.

... FIGHTING REPORTED SOUTH AND WEST OF ALGIERS, DESPITE A CEASEFIRE AGREEMENT BETWEEN STRONGMAN, BEN BELLA AND THE GUERRILLA LEADERS OPPOSING HIM...

... IN A STATEMENT LAST NIGHT, PRESIDENT KENNEDY INDICATED THAT THE RECENT SOVIET ACTIVITY HAD BEEN LARGELY DEFENSIVE IN NATURE...

AND, IN LOCAL NEWS...

FREE FROM WORRY ♫♩ FREE FROM CARE ♫♩ IT'S A SECRET YOU'LL WANT TO SHARE! ♫♩ RECOMMENDED BY DOCTORS!

THANKS FOR NOTHING "PARTNER."
~ C'MON... EARLY RETIREMENT. ~ COULDA' BEEN A LOT WORSE...
LONNIE? TOM? ~ WHAT'S GOING ON?

HEH...
DAILY NEWS
NO CLUES IN MANHUNT

...Police are seeking any information that can help identify the criminals in Tuesday's daylight robbery..
THERE YA GO...
SPRING SALE
BROOME COUNTY
GENERAL DIRECTORY
1962

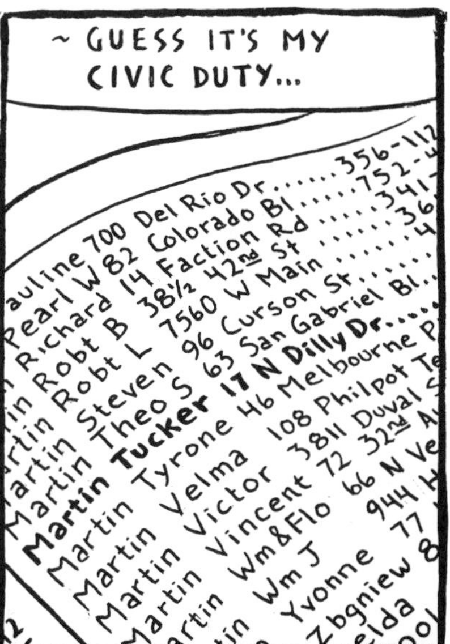
~ GUESS IT'S MY CIVIC DUTY...
auline 700 Del Rio Dr......356-112
Pearl W 82 Colorado Bl.....752-
Richard 14 Faction Rd.....341
Robt B 38½ 42nd St.....36
Martin Robt L 7560 W Main.....4
Martin Steven 96 Curson St.....
Martin Theo S 63 San Gabriel Bl..
Martin Tucker 17 N Dilly Dr.....
Martin Tyrone 46 Melbourne P
Martin Velma 108 Philpot Te
Martin Victor 3811 Duval S
Martin Vincent 72 32nd A
Martin Wm&Flo 66 N Ve
Martin Wm J 944
Yvonne 77
Zbgniew 8
elda

Beautiful
HOMES
$13500 AND UP

SIGH...
NO CLUES IN MANHUNT

EYY~ BIALYS! ~YOU MIND?
FAP
YES. WHAT IS THAT?
GOT THAT LIST OF "TQP" PLATE NUMBERS...
~THERE'S ONLY ABOUT 200 OF 'EM REGISTERED IN THIS COUNTY.
SWELL...

OCTOBER
~GOOD NEWS IS~ MOST OF 'EM ARE ACCOUNTED FOR...
~THERE'S STILL ABOUT 30 WE CAN CHECK UP ON...
ANY LOCAL?

ELEVEN.
LET'S START WITH THOSE.

ON THE BRIGHT SIDE...
~ IT'S LOOKING LIKE RAIN!

RING!

ACCOUNTS. MR. MARTIN-
-TUCK!
ABOUT TIME YOU CALLED!

YEAH-SORRY. IT'S BEEN PRETTY HECTIC, AROUND HERE...

-BUT LISTEN- CAN YOU GET AWAY, THIS AFTERNOON?
DORFMANN'S
NSWEAR

-DUNNO... MAYBE...
WHAT YA GOT IN MIND?

MEET ME AT 722 PINE ST.
722 PINE 4
IT'S ON BEEKER HILL.

THIS BETTER BE GOOD...

I GOT A FEW **THOUSAND** CLUES, RIGHT HERE IN MY **HAND!**

"WON IT AT THE TRACK!?"

HEY!
BAM!

THAT'S ENOUGH! ~DON'T MAKE ME~
YOU!

I'M GONNA-
-OW! FUCK!
PAF!
ESTHER...
YOU DID THIS!

GODDAMMIT, WOMAN! CUT THIS SHIT OUT!
YOU BRANG THIS DIRTY BUSINESS INTO OUR HOME!

INTO-OUR-HOME!

WHOOP~ SORRY BUDDY. HEY! FERG!
~WHA? LONNIE!
METROPOLITAN SUN DAILY NEWS
MAYOR DENIE ALLEGATI

WHATCHA DOIN'?
~GRABBING A PAPER ON MY WAY HOME.
~YOU JUST GET OFF?
YOU KNOW IT, BROTHER.

SAY~ YA WANNA GRAB THAT BEER?
IT'S NOT TOO EARLY FOR YA?
TATTLER

IT'S **NEVER** TOO EARLY FOR BEER!

Terminal BAR
CAFE
HI-HAT Lounge
TOPLESS
DANCING
BAR
ACE
WALK
SO ~ THIS BANK THING...

~WHO'S ON IT?
~OH ~ IT'S, UH ... IT'S TOM JUREWICZ...
HUH ~ SONUVAGUN ~
WHO'S HE PARTNERED WITH, NOWADAYS?
SCRATCH SCRATCH

YOU REMEMBER SAL ANDRETTI?
SURE SURE, NICE GUY...
ANDRETTI, WHATTAYAKNOW...
ANY NEWS?

WELL... THEY MIGHT HAVE A LEAD ON THE CAR...
YEAH?

OH~ I GOT RID OF THAT CAR A YEAR AGO...

~AND IT WASN'T A GREEN BUICK ~ IT WAS A BLUE DESOTO! MY SON SOLD IT TO A COLORED JUNKMAN, LAST FEBRUARY...

~NO ~ I TELL A LIE ~ IT WASN'T FEBRUARY AT ALL ~ IT WAS **MARCH.** BECAUSE HE GOT ME A NEW CAR FOR MY **BIRTHDAY!**
~MY BIRTHDAY'S IN MARCH, YOU SEE...

~AND THIS JUNKMAN, MA'AM... DO YOU HAVE THAT ADDRESS?

HEAVENS NO! MY SON WOULD KNOW ALL THAT...
~MARCH IS THE SIGN OF THE **FISH**... WHICH I DON'T THINK IS NICE **AT ALL** ~ DON'T YOU AGREE?...
YOUR SON, MA'AM ~ HOW COULD WE GET IN TOUCH WITH HIM?

ERSON'S
PIANO
VICE RENTAL
Steinway
Baumgardt
Clementi
Lesage
Perzol
SANFORD'S. ~IT'S OVER IN BUTCHERTOWN.
Hammonds
Candy Express
LLT411
AND THIS WAS OVER A YEAR AGO?
DID YOU SIGN A TRANSFER?
EHH...

ESTHER...
NO! I AM **NOT** HAVING THIS IN OUR HOME!

AND WE **BETTER** NOT BE HAVING THIS CONVERSATION **AGAIN!** I AM **DONE** WITH THIS!

NOW YOU JUST HOLD ON ONE MINUTE...
THIS **BETTER** BE GONE TIME I GET BACK!

WOMAN, WHO YOU THINK-
YOU HEARD ME!

SLAM!

WHO THAT FOOL THINK HE IS TRY TO LIE TO ME?
~I WILL **NOT** HAVE THAT MESS POLLUTING MY HOME.
~NO MA'AM, I WILL **NOT**...

PLUMBING
HARDWARE

722
PINE

OH, DON'T HURRY...
I'VE GOT ALL DAY TO WAIT A ROUND FOR YOU...

SORRY TO BE SO LATE. MEETING RAN LONG...
MHM.
~HERE~ LET ME MAKE IT UP TO YOU!

GOING UP!

WHAT IS THIS?
TRY IT OUT!

AFTER YOU!
A

HERE WE ARE...

OUR OWN LITTLE "PIED-A-TERRE" RIGHT HERE IN THE CITY...
NO MORE HOTEL ROOMS FOR US!

IT'S GOT A FULLY-STOCKED BAR, TV, HI-FI SYSTEM, A VIEW OF DOWNTOWN...

~ WHAT DO YOU THINK?

HAS IT GOT A BEDROOM?

SANFORD AUTO SAL
AUTO
SALVAGE
PARTS

CLINKITY CLINKITY
WHAT THE HELL?

CLINKITY CLINKITY CLINK
TOM...
OH...

RAAWWR-IPE!

BUNG!
SHIT!

JESUS, MARY & JOSEPH!
RATTLE
SHAKE

HELLO?
GRRRRRRR...

GRRRRR...

OKAY-SO NOBODY HOME...
ROWF!
ROWF!

IT'S GONNA RAIN ANY MINUTE. WHAT SAY WE GET LUNCH?
HOLD ON A SEC...

PATROLMAN!

RUMBLE

FRIGGIN' GREAT...

SHE LOOKS LIKE A REAL HANDFUL!
WHATCHOO WANT, MAN?

NOTHIN'...
~A DRINK.

YOU LET THAT RAGWEED GET A FOOTHOLD...
IT'LL BE UP ONTO YER PORCH BEFORE YA KNOW IT.

MMMMM...

?

AHEM...

WHAT'S GOING ON, DOWN THERE?

~ER...
AH...
SORRY...

I GUESS I'M NOT REALLY MYSELF, LATELY.

YEAH? WHO ARE YA, NOW? ~GOTTA SAY~ I LIKE THE OTHER ONE BETTER.

IT'S JUST THIS ROBBERY...

WORK'S A MADHOUSE ~ THE CFO IS BREATHING DOWN MY NECK...
~AND THE POLICE...

~I CAN'T BE SURE, BUT FROM THEIR QUESTIONS IT SOUNDED LIKE THEY MIGHT THINK I HAD SOMETHING TO DO WITH IT...
WELL, DIDJA?

NO! OF COURSE NOT!
THEN YA GOT NOTHING TO WORRY ABOUT, RIGHT?
RELAX, FOR CHRISSAKES...
I'LL MAKE US A DRINK.

THERE YOU GO ~ AND LOOK...
FOR THE RAIN.
TINK
SAY ~ DID YOU REALLY THINK I WOULD DO A THING LIKE THAT?
MUCH.
FEEL BETTER NOW?
WHY NOT? IT'S A LOTTA MONEY ~ YOU'VE GOT EXPENSES ~ BESIDES...

~ YOU'RE NOT SO PURE!
FOOLING AROUND WITH A MARRIED WOMAN...
TOO TRUE! ~ HEH ~ GUILTY AS CHARGED...

ALL THE PIZAZZ AND NO TIES...
EVERY MAN'S DREAM, RIGHT?

HEY, NOW...
~ IT'S ALL RIGHT, TUCK ~ I'M A BIG GIRL. I KNOW THE SCORE. I KNOW IT'S NEVER GONNA HAPPEN...
~ I'M **CATHOLIC** FOR ONE THING...
BAD AS IT IS?
I GOTTA STICK IT OUT TO THE END OF THE LINE.

IS IT BAD?
~I MEAN~ WE'VE NEVER TALKED ABOUT IT... ~YOUR MARRIAGE.
WELL, WE SURE AREN'T GONNA START, NOW!
LET'S JUST SAY IT'S BEEN... UNDERWHELMING AND LEAVE IT AT THAT...

A LOTTA BIG TALK THAT WENT NOWHERE...
END OF STORY.

SO...
SPEAKING OF DISAPPOINTMENT.
WANNA GIVE IT ANOTHER SHOT, STUD?
I, UH... ~HEH~
NEVERMIND...
FORGET IT.

DR MAC
TAX
SERVICE
while u wait!
NOTARY
PUBLIC
licenced
bonded
BILLIARDS
RAV
8
BAL

RED ~ SOME FOLKS WANT TO TALK TO YOU ABOUT SOMETHING...
H'LO, BABE.
CHARLES.

WHAT FOLKS?
TALK ABOUT WHAT?
OH...
I PROB'LY GOT NOTHIN' TO SAY...
RELAX. WE'RE JUST LOOKING FOR A CAR.

WHAZZAT? POLICE NEED A CAR? ~ AND THEY COMIN' TO ME?

HA
HA HA
MUST BE HARD TIMES FOR THE POLICE!
HA HA
HA HA
HA
HA
HA

RUMBLE
~ SO, THOSE PLATES ~ WHERE'D YOU GET EM?
~ THAT'S WHAT YOU COME OUT HERE FOR?

INDULGE ME ~ WHERE?

YARD WHERE I WORK. THERE'S 100 FUCKIN' CARS OUT THERE.
TOOK EM OFF AN OLD DESOTO.

UH-HUH...
-AND THE CAR WE USED FOR THE JOB...

-WHERE'D YOU DITCH THAT?
THAT A TRICK QUESTION?

IT'S AT THE YARD ~ A WEEK'S TIME, IT'LL BE PARTED OUT.
DONE AND DONE.

~ YOU HAPPY NOW?

LEMME GET THIS STRAIGHT...
~YOU USED PLATES FROM A SALVAGE YARD...
~DUMPED THE CAR AT THE SAME SALVAGE YARD...
POSTIES

~THE YARD WHERE YOU WORK...
~IS THAT RIGHT?

WHAT?

JESUS, BOY...

YOU DON'T COME INTO MY HOUSE ~ DRINK MY LIQUOR, AND CALL ME NOTHIN'!

YOU ABOUT 5 SECONDS AWAY FROM-

HEH, HEH!

OW!

DAMMIT!

FLICK

AAAA!
BAMB!

HUH!

MPH - FUCKER...

CHUNK!

OKAY...

THAT'S IT FOR YOU...
NOW WHAT?

SNAP

OH YEAH...

HEH

THERE YA GO...

GOT ALL THE WAY TO GRANDVIEW
'FOR I REMEMBERED THEY CLOSED ON~

GASP!

EEEEK!

OH, GODDAMMIT...

EEEEEEEEK!

HELP! OH HELP ME!

CRASH!

BUMP!

~MPH!
WHALP!

GUH!
CLUNK

CHRIST...
~WHAT NEXT?

OKAY THEN...

SORRY, SISTER...

~ WRONG PLACE. WRONG TIME...
-MMN...

KNOCK KNOCK!
WHAT'S GOING ON IN THERE?
?!

~ESTHER! I HEARD A RUCKUS ~ YOU ALRIGHT?
I'M COMIN' IN THERE!
KNOCK KNOCK!

~ GOTTA BE KIDDIN' ME...

WHO'S THAT THERE?

OH MY LORD...
UH...

~ SOMEBODY CALL THE POLICE!

THERE YOU GO...
RRRRRRRRRRRRR

~BLUE DESOTO. JUST LIKE YOU ASK.
YEAH ~ WHERE ARE THE PLATES FOR THIS HEAP?

SUPPOSED TO BE ON THE CAR...
AIN'T THEY THERE?

DOES IT LOOK LIKE IT TO YOU?
I CAN'T SEE NOTHIN' WITHOUT MY SPECS!
~WHERE'D I PUT 'EM NOW? LEMME SEE, UH...
BINGO!

~I DON'T KNOW NOTHIN' ABOUT THAT...

~YOU ASK CALVIN ABOUT THAT SHIT!

CALVIN?

THIS IS IT.
THE HELL YOU SAY...

LANSKY. WHAT GIVES?
HOMOCIDE.
~DOMESTIC, LOOKS LIKE...
~NOW WHAT BRINGS YOU BOYS ACROSS THE RIVER?
I **TOLD** YOU ~ I SEEN A WHITE MAN, RUNNING OUT THE BACK DOOR! WHY AIN'T YOU OUT LOOKING FOR HIM?
CAN YOU DESCRIBE HIM, MA'AM?
WE'RE LOOKING FOR A CALVIN JULIUS ~ ON THE FIRST FEDERAL THING.
YEAH? WELL, HE'S IN THERE, ALRIGHT...
~DUNNO HOW **COOPERATIVE** HE'S GONNA' BE...

SO WHAT DO YOU THINK?

NEITHER ONE OF THE GUYS INSIDE THE BANK WAS COLORED...
IF THIS GUY'S INVOLVED, HE'S MAYBE THE DRIVER...
AND?
~SO WHAT'S HE DOING WITH THIS PISTOL?
I DUNNO. ASK HIM.
WHAT'S THE DIFF?

MAYBE NOTHING... IT'S JUST FUNNY, IS ALL...
SOMETHING'S NOT RIGHT, HERE...

YOU THINK THAT'S FUNNY, THIS'LL KILL YA...

TUCKER FRIGGIN' MARTIN...
LIEUTENANT...

~THERE'S NO SIGN OF ANY CASH...

SO... YOU BOYS ABOUT DONE IN HERE?

RAIN'S LETTING UP.

FIELDING Co
Be Refreshed
CHEW
DOUBLEMINT
GUM
ROOMS

Fairhurst
Automotive
SAJ 311

I DIDN'T MARRY YOU SO I COULD GO BACK TO WORK.
IT'S JUST TEMPORARY TIL I GET BACK ON MY FEET. ~BESIDES, IT'LL GET YA OUT OF THE HOUSE, RIGHT?
SSIFIEDS

WHAM!
WHOA!
LOOK AT YOU! THE COMEBACK KID, HERE...
WATCH AND LEARN.
LUCK!
SCIENCE...
Gus
Lonnie

FRIDAY: LADI
IT'S ALL ABOUT CONTROL...
ROSS'S RULE NUMBER ONE: LEAVE NOTHING TO CHANCE...
NO LOOSE ENDS.

THAT'S HOW YOU WIN.

BAM!

OUTCOME WAS NEVER IN DOUBT.

SO, WHAT WERE YOU TWO TALKING ABOUT FOR SO LONG, OVER THERE?
ROXY
HATARI

SINCE WHEN DO YOU CARE?
YOU WERE TALKING ABOUT SHOES... SHOES AND MAKEUP, AMIRIGHT?...

⁼SIGH⁼ JUNE SAYS GUS IS UNHAPPY AT WORK...
~FEELS HE'S BEING PASSED OVER FOR SOME NEW KID WHO KNOWS SOMEBODY...
I DUNNO...

I WASN'T REALLY PAYING ATTENTION, YOU WANNA KNOW THE TRUTH.

YEAH~WELL~ MAYBE THAT'S GUS'S PROBLEM...
MN?

ATTENTION...
YOU GOTTA STAY SHARP, YOU WANNA MAKE IT IN THIS WORLD...
YUM-YUM
YUM-YUM
HAMBURGERS
MILKSHAKES
SAJ 311

EXPECT THE UNEXPECTED...
BE FLEXIBLE...
ADAPT.
~GOTTA KEEP YER EYES OPEN AND BE READY FOR WHATEVER...
TELLING YA...
THAT'S HOW YOU STAY A STEP AHEAD OF THE OTHER GUY.

THAT'S HOW YOU KEEP CONTROL OF ANY SITUATION.

≡SNORT≡ LIKE YOU KNOW SO MUCH ABOUT IT.

YOU'D BE SURPRISED THE THINGS I KNOW...
YOU'RE RIGHT. I WOULD BE!
SHEESH...

MR. BIGSTUFF, HERE...

17

17
17
LBC670

Ford

DILLY DR
US MAIL

HELLO, POLICE?

I DON'T KNOW WHO THAT MAN WAS, BUT I BET THAT ROY HAD SOMETHIN' TO DO WITH IT...
ROY? HE HAVE A LAST NAME?
1962

POTTER~ROY POTTER.

I KNEW THEY WAS UP TO NO GOOD...

POTTER...Y'KNOW~ I THINK I KNOW THIS GUY FROM WHEN I WORKED VICE...
~BEATNIK.
~JUNKIE...
~LIVES IN THE VILLAGE.

RECORD?
PICAYUNE SHIT. NEVER HEARD HE GOT UP TO ANYTHING ALONG THESE LINES...

FINALLY DECIDES TO MAKE SOMETHING OF HIMSELF.
~THAT'S THE SPIRIT!
~HEM.

YOU BOYS ARE WORKING THAT BANK JOB, RIGHT?
YEAH, WHY?

I SOLVED IT FOR YA - THE MONEY'S AT THE HOME OF ONE "TUCKER MARTIN", IN TARRYTOWN...
HERE'S THE ADDRESS.
~ KIDDIN' ME.

WHERE'D YOU GET THIS?
DIDN'T LEAVE THEIR NAME, BUT I THINK IT'S SAFE TO SAY IT WASN'T LADYBIRD JOHNSON...

WELL... AIN'T THAT A KICK IN THE PANTS?
I'LL TALK TO THE CAPTAIN, ~BETWEEN THAT CARD AND THIS TIP, WE SHOULD BE GOLD FOR A SEARCH-WARRANT...

WE'LL BRING MARTIN IN, ANY RATE ~ SEE IF MISS WATSON HERE, CAN PICK HIM OUT...

~ MEANTIME, YOU GO SEE IF YOU CAN FIND THE BEATNIK.
~ TRY MAME'S, OR THE PARK, MAYBE...

I WANT YOU
FOR U.S. ARMY
LIVE
AT THE
ROXY!

UP AND AT 'EM BROTHER~ BILLS TO PAY...
ALWAYS, ALWAYS...
HE VOICE
ALL GUESTS

ES
1713
1715 Kober 1715
PHOTO STUDIO
LOUIS
CANDY
STORE
PEPSI
SHAVED ICE
ENTRANCE
OPEN FROM
10AM TO 3AM
AIR CONDITIONED
Liquor Served
Dover CLEANER
WE SP

EMPLOYEE OF THE MONTH

NOTICE

THERE ARE SOME PEOPLE TO SEE YOU...

NOT NOW, ALICE... ~I NEED~

WHERE IS THE MITCHELL ACCOUNT?

~BUT MR. MARTIN...

THIS IS **LAST** QUARTER'S... ~

REGULAR BEAR GARDEN, AROUND HERE, LATELY

MR MARTIN, **TUCK!**

OH DEAR!

WE'D LIKE A WORD.

DANCE
MAGAZINES · PERIO
NEW & USED BOOKS · GIFT
NEWS
SODAS · CIGARETTES · CANDY
LUNCHEONETTE
SANDWICHES · HOT DOGS · ICE CREAM
MENU
1426
SEAN CONNER
DR NO
SLOW
CIRCUS OF BOOKS
OPEN
HOT DOG
15¢
TAXI
P07131

POETRY READING
GASLIGHT
Gaslight
CAFE
AFRICAN HERITAGE

ROY~ MY MAN! WHAT IS COOKING TODAY?
BLOOP
STONE SOUP...

IT'S AN OLD FAMILY RECIPE...

DOUBLE-DOUBLE TOIL AND TROUBLE...
STONED SOUP, HUH? ~THAT SOUND LIKE MY KIND OF SOUP!
HEH.
SAY MAN...
YOU THINK I COULD GET ME A TASTE?

WELL... THE SOUP'S NOT READY, BUT, I TELL YOU WHAT, IRVING...
LIVE & IN-PERSON
ZAZOU COWBOYS

I GOT SOMETHING ELSE YOU MIGHT LIKE...

AW, YOU KNOW THAT I DO!
~THANK YOU, MY BROTHER!
~HEY UH...
~I HEARD ABOUT CALVIN, MAN. REAL SORRY ABOUT THAT...
I KNOW YOU WAS TIGHT.
WHAT?
WHAT ABOUT HIM?

YOU AIN'T HEARD? HE'S DEAD, MAN!

~ICED WITH A KNIFE!

SAY WHAT?!
WHERE'D YOU HEAR THAT?!
SORRY, BROTHER, THOUGHT YOU KNEW...
HEAT'S ON, DADDY-O!

HUH?
THE FUZZ...
THE CONSTABULARY.
THE MAN, WITH THE STAR, ON THE CAR.

BETTER SPLIT, MAN... HE'S ASKING FOR YOU!
~THE HELL?

SHE SAID THERE'D BE DAYS LIKE THIS...

ARLO, YOU'RE A MENSCH,
FLOOP
HEY, CONGRATS...
~IRVING, YOU'RE THE NEW HEAD CHEF.

SO, WHAT'S FOR DINNER?
STONED SOUP!

SLAM!
?

YOU'RE HOME, EARLY... WHAT~ YA GET FIRED FOR STEALING PAPERCLIPS?
THAT'S FRIGGIN' HILARIOUS, COMING FROM YOU.

AS A MATTER OF FACT IT'S A JEWISH HOLIDAY.
SIMCHAT SOMETHING...

ANYHOW, SID ISN'T ALLOWED TO WORK, SO THERE WAS NOTHING FOR ME TO DO.
SO, I LEFT.

I'M GONNA TAKE A BATH.
I'M MEETING THE GIRLS TONIGHT, SO...

MEETING "THE GIRLS"...
GOOD LUCK WITH THAT...

~I GOT A FEELING THEY MIGHT HAVE TO CANCEL ON YOU, TONIGHT.
WHAT'S THIS ALL ABOUT?
2
3
4
5

WELL... IT AIN'T MISTER THREE ~ HE'S TOO TALL.

~AND MISTER FIVE? HE'S TOO FAT, BUT...
TAKE YOUR TIME...

NAH~ NOTHIN' YET. ~YOU WANT I SHOULD STICK ON HIS LAST KNOWN?

NO, FORGET POTTER FOR NOW AND GET OVER TO TARRYTOWN...
WE'RE GOOD TO GO FOR THE MARTIN RESIDENCE.

THE GIRL?
NUMBER TWO ~ TAKE ONE STEP FORWARD.

TO BE HONEST? WHITE FOLKS ALL KINDA' LOOK THE SAME...
~WE'RE WORKING ON IT...

CAFETERIA
NEWS
CHELSEA

SEELY BROS
TELE
BROUWER PARK

YEAH?
ROY~YOU SOUND AGITATED~DON'T TELL ME YOU SPENT ALL THAT MONEY...
HUH?
NO~HOW WOULD I HAVE HEARD THAT?
~WHEN DID ALL THIS HAPPEN?
JEEZ...
WITH A KNIFE, HUH? THAT'S TOUGH.
~STILL, A GUY LIKE THAT.
~YOU KNOW WHAT I MEAN...

NO~YER RIGHT. I'M SURE HE WAS A PILLAR OF HIS COMMUNITY...
HE'LL BE MISSED...
THE POLICE? NO... YOU GOT NOTHIN' TO WORRY ABOUT, THERE.
SETTLE DOWN, FOR CHRISSAKES!
SO WHAT IF THEY DO?
~SO, YOU KNEW THE GUY_ SO WHAT?
KNOWING A DEAD GUY DOESN'T MEAN ANYTHING...
USE YER HEAD.

YEAH~THEY MIGHT TIE HIM TO THE JOB~BUT WE'RE CLEAR!

NOTHING CONNECTS US.
~SURE, I'M SURE~BESIDES...

I GOT THIS COVERED.
~SET UP A PATSY TO TAKE THE FALL.

I REPEAT ~ MY CLIENT HAS NOTHING FURTHER TO SAY. ~ IF THERE ARE NO FORMAL CHARGES...

HEY NOW... THIS IS JUST A FRIENDLY CONVERSATION!

I DUNNO, LONNIE ~ I THINK YOU MAY BE UNDERESTIMATING THE POLICE, HERE.
~NOT FOR THE FIRST TIME, I MIGHT ADD...
LISTEN, ROY, I KNOW THESE GUYS...

~I KNOW HOW THEY THINK BELIEVE ME...
?

~I'VE GOT ALL THE ANGLES COVERED...
WHAT THE HELL?

WHAT?! WHAT IS WHAT? ~ LONNIE?...
CLUNK

722 PINE 4

GODDAMMIT...

MEETING THE GIRLS?...
HEY! PRIVACY!

GETTIN' ALL CLEAN FOR BINGO NIGHT?

WHAT THE HELL KINDA' QUESTION IS THAT? ~ FRANKLY, IT'S NONE OF YOUR BUSINESS WHAT I DO!
NOW, IF YOU DON'T MIND, I'D LIKE~

NONE OF MY BUSINESS, HUH?
BLOOSH!

SPLOSHA
THUMP!
BUMP!

WHOA!
~HEH HEH...
SWIPE

EHH...
GASP!

FUCK BINGO NIGHT.
COUGH!

HAVE YOU LOST YOUR COUGH YOUR GODDAMNED MIND?!
~YOU THINK THAT'S FRIGGIN' FUNNY?

COUGH
GASP

COUGH
YOU SON OF A BITCH...

WHAT, YOU GOT NOTHING TO SAY? ~JUST DROWN YOUR WIFE AND WALK OUTTA' HERE?
I'M TAKING THE CAR.

I HOPE YOU FRIGGIN' CRASH IT OFF A BRIDGE, YOU LOUSY BASTARD!

SLAM!

722
PINE
4

YEAH ~ IN AN OVERNIGHT BAG, IN THE GARAGE...
IT'S NOTHIN' LIKE THE WHOLE TAKE, ~ BUT AT LEAST IT'S A START, RIGHT?

TAXI!
EPHONE

IF THE SERIAL NUMBERS MATCH, IT'S ENOUGH. ~ BUT MORE IS ALWAYS BETTER ~ SEE WHAT ELSE YOU CAN DIG UP...
MPD

REMEMBER: DONT TALK TO ANYONE ABOUT THIS, WITHOUT MY SAY SO...
PARK
LBC670

FLORIST
RIST
OPEN

KATE?
...
HUH...

WHAT ARE YOU DOING HERE, ROY?

I GOTTA TALK TO LONNIE...

HE CAN GO TO HELL...

~YOU, TOO.

WAIT!

C'MON ~ IT'S IMPORTANT!

YEAH? ~THAT WAS YOU ON THE PHONE WITH HIM, EARLIER, RIGHT?

~WELL, YA MISSED HIM... FLEW OUTTA' HERE LIKE HIS PANTS WERE ON FIRE...
~YOU MUSTA' SAID SOMETHING PRETTY SPECIAL.
~I, UM...

HE **ATTACKED** ME, ROY... ~TRIED TO **DROWN** ME...
~I GOT YOU TO THANK FOR THAT, TOO?
WHAT?
NO!

~ KATE, I WOULD **NEVER**...
~ARE YOU OKAY?
DID HE HURT YOU? ~I'LL...

ALRIGHT ...
EASY, TIGER ...
MAYBE YOU BETTER COME INSIDE, HUH?

SO...

WHAT'S GOT YOU SO HOT AND BOTHERED?
UH ~ I DUNNO IF I SHOULD ~ I MEAN, LONNIE...

OH, C'MON ROY ~ SPILL IT...

YOU TWO ARE OBVIOUSLY UP TO SOMETHING ~ AND FROM THE LOOKS OF IT, THINGS HAVE GOTTEN OUT OF HAND.

~ BIG FRIGGIN' SURPRISE...

~ SO, TELL ME HEPCAT...

WHAT'S THE BIG SECRET?
WELL...

~SO, YOU'RE TELLING ME, NOW THIS CALVIN PERSON IS DEAD AND THE POLICE ARE AFTER YOU?
~THAT ABOUT THE SIZE OF IT?
~JESUS, YOU TWO...
YOUR LITTLE IMPOUNDED-DOPE SHENANIGANS WERE BAD ENOUGH, BUT THIS...
THIS IS A WHOLE NEW LEVEL OF STUPID!

LONNIE SAYS IT'S ALL UNDER CONTROL, BUT ~ NO OFFENSE, BUT YOU KNOW HOW HE IS...
~OH - BELIEVE ME ~ I KNOW...

APPARENTLY, HE HAS SOME POOR BASTARD SET UP TO TAKE THE FALL FOR THIS, BUT I DUNNO HOW MUCH OF THAT IS TRUE, AND HOW MUCH IS JUST...

...LONNIE BEING LONNIE...
722 PINE

LISTEN, ROY...
THIS IS...
~I DUNNO **WHAT** THIS IS...

~I GOTTA' LOT TO THINK ABOUT, HERE.
~MAYBE YOU SHOULD COME BACK LATER, HUH?
~BUT LONNIE...
HE'LL BE BACK LATER~YOU CAN SEE HIM, THEN.
~OR NOT. I DON'T CARE.
BUT
SLAM!

HOLY MOTHER OF GOD.

RING!

IT'S ME. ~SIGH... I KNOW WHO ROBBED YOUR BANK.

...YOU CAN'T BE SERIOUS...

~ YOUR HUSBAND DID THIS?
HE MUST HAVE FOUND OUT ABOUT US...

~ THIS IS HIS WAY OF DEALING WITH IT.

KATE, ARE YOU 100% SURE? I MEAN MAYBE... I DUNNO...
YUP. PRETTY SURE.

SIGH
THIS EXPLAINS A LOT...

CHRIST, WHAT A MESS...
~YOU'LL PROBABLY LOSE YOUR JOB...

WE BOTH WILL...
~BEATS PRISON...
~WHERE MY HUSBAND WILL BE GOING...

KATE...
~DON'T GET ME WRONG, ~BETTER HIM THAN YOU...
~BUT STILL. I DIDN'T HAVE TO MAKE THIS CALL...
YOU OWE ME FOR THIS, TUCK.

I KNOW IT.

WHEN THIS IS ALL OVER... WHAT DO YOU SAY TO CALIFORNIA?

YEAH?

I'LL... THINK ABOUT IT...

5

~SO, IT'S SETTLED, THEN...

~I'LL PICK YOU UP, AND WE'LL GO TO THE STATION TOGETHER...

DING!

4

BOY OH BOY, KATE...

~YOU'VE GOT THIS CHUMP HOOKED, ALL RIGHT...

SO FAR, SO GOOD...

UH OH...

YEAH?

DID YOU KNOW THIS GUY HAD A SECOND ADDRESS? ~ RIGHT IN MIDTOWN...

–?

–!

OH, JESUS!

SNAP!
722
PINE

Lonnie
Ross
John Co.
Security

~THIS CAN'T BE GOOD...

CLICK

HOLD IT RIGHT THERE!
YOU!
~HEH... HELLO, TUCK.

YOU... YOU'RE KATE'S HUSBAND?
HORNS AND ALL!
WHAT ~ UM... WHAT ARE YOU DOING, HERE?

PLAYING CATCH-UP! JUST FOUND OUT ABOUT YER LITTLE LOVE NEST, THIS AFTERNOON...

~ CAME HERE TO CLEAR IT OF ANYTHING MIGHT CONNECT YOU TO KATE, WHEN THE COPS TUMBLE TO THIS PLACE...

~ AND I FIND THIS NOTE WITH MY NAME ON IT...
~ AND I'M THINKING WHAT BAD NEWS THIS IS FOR ME...

~ AND NOW YOU WALK IN!
~ AND HERE WE ARE...

~ SO I GUESS THE SIXTY-FOUR DOLLAR QUESTION IS...

~ WHAT HAPPENS NEXT?

RINNG!

WHOP!
OW!
CLANG!

GODDAMMIT!
BANG!
HELLO? TUCK?

POW!

FLUMP!

CREAK

SLAM!

SNATCH

SNICK

LOOKS LIKE HE'S HOME...
722 PINE

OKAY, TUCK...
UMPH
UPSY-DAISY!

?

!

SHIT!

DON'T WANT HIM SLIPPING PAST US ~ I'LL TAKE THIS...
~ YOU GET THE STAIRS.
JEEZ, THANKS.
~ DON'T MENTION IT.

OOF
C'MON, BUDDY...
~EASY DOES IT...

MR. MARTIN? POLICE! OPEN UP!
BAM BAM!
HUFF
PUFF

C'MON, TUCK ~ WE DON'T HAVE ALL DAY...

HELLO?
IS IT SAFE?
IS HE GONE?

WHUMP!

SHOTS? HOW MANY SHOTS?
WHEN DID THIS HAPPEN?
JUST A MINUTE AGO~BUT LOOK...
~DID YOU SEE MR. MARTIN?
I DON'T...
~DID YOU SEE HIM SHOOT SOMEONE?
I DON'T WANNA' GET INVOLVED...

ROOF ACCESS
HE'S GOTTA STILL BE IN THE BUILDING...

LBC670

ROOF ACCESS

TUCK? IT'S TOM JUREWICZ.
~WE'RE COMING OUT THERE...

VROOM!

?
VROOM!

I SEE HIM!
HE'S ON THE STREET!

LBC 670

CRAP...

PUT OUT AN APB - HE WON'T GET FAR IN THAT EASTER EGG...

AUTOS

CAFE ✱ MOTEL
TV

OKAY...

RUMBLE RUMBLE RUMBLE RUMBL-VROOMMOOMMM

POP!
VVVOOMMM!
PASH!

GOODNIGHT, TUCK.

SAN FRANCISCO
GREYHOUND
95
ACME
MANUFACTU

VIN&SONS

YAWN

I KNOW WHAT YOU DID.
TV GUIDE

JEEZ... YER NOT STILL SORE ABOUT GETTING YER HAIR WET?

I HEARD YOU SHOOT HIM, LONNIE... LOOK ME IN THE EYE AND TELL ME I'M WRONG.

... EHH...
~ HE BROUGHT IT ON HIMSELF.

YOU'RE ONE TO TALK...
GIMME THE CAR KEYS.
YOU'RE KIDDIN' ME!

I'M LEAVING YOU, LONNIE.

THIS WONT MAKE UP FOR WHAT YOU DID, BUT IT'LL HAVE TO DO...
WHAT I DID?
YOU STARTED THIS!
OH ~ SO THIS IS MY FAULT?

WHATEVER I DID, I DID IT TO SAVE THIS MARRIAGE!
~IF YOU HADN'T-
YEAH? ROBBERY AND MURDER? ~YOU'RE NOT "SAVING" ANYTHING. ~YOU JUST CAN'T STAND THAT I WAS HAPPY FOR ONCE IN MY GODDAMNED LIFE...
~YOU JUST HAD TO RUIN IT.
CRY ME A RIVER...
I LIKED HIM! ~AND I'M LEAVING! ... SO GIMME THE GODDAMN KEYS!
~CHEATING ON ME WITH THAT SLICK CREAMPUFF!
PUT THAT DOWN! ~YOU'RE NOT WALKING OUT ON ME!

~ AFTER EVERYTHING I'VE -
WE'RE DONE!
HELL WE ARE!
THIS IS MINE!

BLAM!
BOOM!

KAF!

NEVER THOUGHT I'D MARRY A COP.
NEVER THOUGHT I'D MARRY **AT ALL**. ~ BUT YOU... **YOU'RE A KEEPER!**

KING SUSAN
USED CARS
the BEST DEALS WEST of the PECOS!
FREE OIL CHANGE

gsc
2016

Editor: **Gary Groth**
Designer: **Sean David Williams**
Production: **Preston White**
Associate Publisher: **Eric Reynolds**
Publisher: **Gary Groth**

Fantagraphics Books, Inc.
7563 Lake City Way NE
Seattle, WA 98115

To Have and To Hold is copyright © 2017 Graham Chaffee. All rights reserved.
Permission to reproduce materials must be obtained from the author or the publisher.

ISBN: **978-1-60699-988-2**
Library of Congress Control Number: **2016911476**
First Printing: **April, 2017**
Printed in China

ABOUT THE AUTHOR

Graham Chaffee is a professional tattooist and comics artist. His previous books are *The Big Wheels* (1993), *The Most Important Thing & Other Stories* (1995), and *Good Dog* (2013 (all from Fantagraphics Books). He lives and works in Los Angeles.